Larry Burkett's Little Instruction Book

On Managing Your Money

HONOR
BOOKS

Tulsa, Oklahoma

D0452097

Larry Burkett's Little Instruction Book on Managing Your Money
ISBN# 1-56292-152-5
Copyright © 1997 by Christian Financial Concepts, Inc.

All materials taken from works previously published by Moody Press
820 N. LaSalle Boulevard
Chicago, Illinois 60610

This format published by Honor Books
P. O. Box 55388
Tulsa, Oklahoma 74155

Compiled by James S. Bell, Jr.

Introduction

God never intended for Christians to be the poor of the world, but rather to be a testimony of His blessings. However, to be "blessed in the city," and "blessed in the field," is not automatic (Deuteronomy 28:3). It requires training and discipline. These two elements are found in God's Word, the *Holy Bible*.

In this compact volume you will find that the insights of God's Word contain the principles for a solid personal financial foundation. As you gain insight concerning your finances, it is our hope that you will become a living example of God's blessings as you live according to His Word.

Out of gratitude for God's blessings on your life may you become a "giver" to many as an example of His love.

Bailing Out Of The Boat

Consider every decision on the basis of its effect on the work and reputation of Christ. Do not put God into a financial corner and place Him in the role of a "bailer"; I suspect God does not like to sit in the back of a leaky boat and continually have to bail us out.

Whether, then, you eat or drink or whatever you do, do all to the glory of God.

1 Corinthians 10:31

Employment Makes The Difference

The difference between a recession and a depression is whether you are employed.

A little sleep, a little slumber, a little folding of the hands to rest—and poverty will come on you like a bandit and scarcity like an armed man.

Proverbs 6:10,11 NIV

Financial Freedom

Financial freedom is relief from
worry and tension about overdue bills, a clear
conscience before God and others, and the
absolute assurance that God is in
control of your finances.

---

*Honor the Lord from your wealth, and
from the first of all your produce; so your barns
will be filled with plenty, and your vats
will overflow with new wine.*

Proverbs 3:9,10

Earthly Parables

The attraction of materialism is so
great that Christ devoted two-thirds
of His parables to warning His
disciples about it.

---

*Love not the world, neither the things that
are in the world. If any man love the world,
the love of the Father is not in him.*

1 John 2:15 KJV

The Name Is Quality

What a great witness it would be if
every time customers encountered
Christian-run companies what they
would remember would be the quality.

---

*A good name is to be more
desired than great riches, favor
is better than silver and gold.*

Proverbs 22:1

Who Envies Whom?

Most people who are trapped in
prestigious, well-paying jobs that do
not meet their inner needs spend their
lives envying the very people who
are envying them.

---

*There is one who pretends to be rich,
but has nothing; another pretends to
be poor, but has great wealth.*

Proverbs 13:7

A Lender Be

God's Word tells us that His plan for us is to be
debt-free. And even better, we should be
lenders rather than borrowers.

---

*The Lord will open for you His good
storehouse, the heavens, to give rain to
your land in its season and to bless all
the work of your hand; and you shall lend to
many nations, but you shall not borrow.*

Deuteronomy 28:12

Gratitude Over Worry

It's hard to make ourselves stop worrying, but we can decide to ask God for what we want, thank Him for what He's already given, and thank Him for being the kind of good Father who gives good gifts to His children. Cultivating gratitude reminds us that God is good and, therefore, we don't need to worry.

If you then, being evil, know how to give good gifts to your children, how much more shall your Father who is in heaven give what is good to those who ask Him!

Matthew 7:11

Giving Is A Gift

Some Christians have received a
gift of giving. To them the multiplication
of material worth is an extension of their
basic ministry within the Body of Christ.

---

*We have different gifts, according to the grace
given us...if it is contributing to the needs of
others, let him give generously.*

Romans 12:6,8 NIV

Child-Like Budgets

Every one of our children should learn to live on
reasonable budgets themselves.

---

*Poverty and shame will come to him
who neglects discipline, but he who
regards reproof will be honored.*

Proverbs 13:18

Financial Example

Where are our children to learn good financial
principles if not from us?

---

*Train up a child in the way he
should go, even when he is old
he will not depart from it.*

Proverbs 22:6

Economic Symptoms

Many of the symptoms we see so abundant today—business failures, massive bankruptcies, divorce, and two-job families—stem back to the same basic problem of ignoring God's Word and His warnings.

Now it shall be, if you will diligently obey the Lord your God, being careful to do all His commandments which I command you today, the Lord your God will set you high above all the nations of the earth.

Deuteronomy 28:1

The Wrong Elevator

Pride is the desire to be elevated
because of material achievements.

---

*Instruct those who are rich in this
present world not to be conceited or
to fix their hope on the uncertainty of
riches, but on God, who richly supplies
us with all things to enjoy.*

1 Timothy 6:17

Voluntary Service

We are supposed to acknowledge Jesus
as the rightful owner of the resources
we manage. The time will come when
this chance to acknowledge Jesus
voluntarily is past, but until then we
all get to make daily choices.

---

*For the earth is the Lord's,
and everything in it.*

1 Corinthians 10:26 NIV

It's In God's Name

A Christian must transfer ownership
of every possession to God. That
means money, time, family, material
possessions, education—even earning potential
for the future.

---

*And everyone who has left houses
or brothers or sisters or father or
mother or children or farms for My
name's sake, shall receive many times
as much, and shall inherit eternal life.*

Matthew 19:29

Money And Trust

God will use money to develop
our trustworthiness. This principle
is important because our lives revolve
around the making, spending, saving,
and other uses of money.

---

*If therefore you have not been faithful
in the use of unrighteous mammon,
who will entrust the true riches to you?*

Luke 16:11

Happiness Is Not Expensive

The idea that money brings happiness
is a myth. There is no relationship
between money and happiness.

---

*But godliness with contentment
is great gain.*

1 Timothy 6:6 NIV

Knowledgeable Applications

What are the essential elements in
making sound financial decisions? Adequate
knowledge and the wisdom to apply it.

And wisdom and knowledge
shall be the stability of thy times,
and strength of salvation.

Isaiah 33:6 KJV

Our Work Is A Witness

Few Christians who view their
work as a chore have much of a
witness on or off the job.

Do you see a man skilled in his work?
He will stand before kings; he will not stand
before obscure men.

Proverbs 22:29

Important Fact

Today it is not unusual for a young couple to owe nearly $100,000 within the first two years of marriage.

Prayer And Knowledge

Diligent prayer about specific decisions is no
substitute for a basic working knowledge
of God's financial priorities. If we
know the kinds of things God
values a great deal and those He
considers relatively unimportant, many
financial decisions will be fairly obvious.

---

*Do not be anxious then, saying, "What shall we eat?"
or, "What shall we drink?" or, "With what shall
we clothe ourselves?"...for your heavenly Father
knows that you need all these things.*

Matthew 6:31,32

Debt Is Bondage

Maintain the principle of remaining debt-free.
Make every decision on the basis of whether
it may result in bondage.

---

*Owe nothing to anyone except
to love one another.*

Romans 13:8

The Needs Of The Saints

Getting out of debt is not only scriptural, with
many benefits in its own right, but doing so
allows Christians to contribute to
the needs of the saints and to
evangelize the world.

---

*As each one has received a special gift, employ
it in serving one another, as good stewards
of the manifold grace of God.*

1 Peter 4:10

Directed Giving

The most important principle of all
is to allow God to direct your giving.

---

*Trust in the Lord with all thine heart; and lean
not unto thine own understanding. In all
thy ways acknowledge him, and he
shall direct thy paths.*

Proverbs 3:5,6 KJV

Men Spend More

It may be true that women
buy on impulse more often than men,
but when a woman spends impulsively, she will
typically buy a new outfit. When a man takes
the plunge, he will come home with
a new car or boat. Men spend less
often, but when they do they
spend more money.

---

*For wisdom is better than jewels; and all
desirable things can not compare with her.*

Proverbs 8:11

Record Success

In order to maintain an orderly
budget, it is necessary to keep records. This
includes both the previously established home
budget and adequate bank records.

---

*Poor is he who works with a negligent hand,
but the hand of the diligent makes rich.*

Proverbs 10:4

False Bread

An employee who will pad his expense account and rationalize it will eventually pad his income and rationalize that as well.

Bread obtained by falsehood is sweet to a man, but afterward his mouth will be filled with gravel.

Proverbs 20:17

A Fair Wage

Many Christian employers are
guilty of paying some employees less than a
livable wage. To hire someone at such
a low wage is in direct violation of
the principle of fairness.

---

*Do not take advantage of a hired man
who is poor and needy.... Pay him his
wages each day before sunset.*

Deuteronomy 24:14,15 NIV

Desiring And Acquiring

Many Christians get trapped into
operating by the world's wisdom rather than
God's. The world says, "Whatever
you see and desire, acquire!"

---

*But seek for His kingdom, and
these things shall be added to you.*

Luke 12:31

Needs And Contentment

Needs are the purchases
necessary to provide your basic
requirements such as food, clothing, a job,
home, medical coverage, and others.

---

*And if we have food and covering,
with these we shall be content.*

1 Timothy 6:8

Glory Over Profit

The purpose of any
Christian, in business or otherwise,
is to glorify God, not just to make a profit.

---

*Whatever you do, do your work heartily,
as for the Lord rather than for men.*

Colossians 3:23

Management And The Supernatural

Sometimes Christians
seem to believe that God will
bless them supernaturally, while they
ignore every pretense of good management.
If you believe that, you haven't studied God's
Word very thoroughly. God's Word
directs us to think and plan.

The mind of man plans his way,
but the Lord directs his steps.

Proverbs 16:9

36

Operating On Whim

One who is never willing
to sacrifice, never willing to deny
impulses, but constantly seeks to indulge
whimsical desires, will always be in
bondage and frustrated.

He who loves pleasure
will become a poor man; he who
loves wine and oil will not become rich.

Proverbs 21:17

Wanting To Work

Financial bondage exists when
there is no desire for gainful employment.

If anyone will not work, neither let him eat.

2 Thessalonians 3:10

Loss And Gain

God's Word promises that slothfulness
will result in loss, but diligence results in gain.

---

*The soul of the sluggard craves and gets
nothing, but the soul of the
diligent is made fat.*

Proverbs 13:4

The Folly of Envy

Envy is the desire to achieve
based on other people's success.

---

*My steps had almost slipped. For I was
envious of the arrogant, as I saw the
prosperity of the wicked.*

Psalm 73:2,3

Increased Dependence

Do not make plans that
are totally dependent on financial increases.
God's wisdom can be manifest through
a reduction, if necessary,
to redirect our lives.

---

*I know how to get along with humble means,
and I also know how to live in prosperity.*

Philippians 4:12

Unceasing Poor

God's Word says that there will
always be needs in the world around us.

For the poor will never cease to be in the land;
therefore I command you, saying, "You
shall freely open your hand to
your brother, to your needy
and poor in your land."

Deuteronomy 15:11

Budgets Are Fun?

Living on a budget is not only prudent,
but it can be fun. As you have successes
in various areas, share them with others.
Challenge your children as well.

---

*Only give heed to yourself and keep
your soul diligently, lest you forget the things
which your eyes have seen...but make them
known to your sons and your grandsons.*

Deuteronomy 4:9

Living Inheritances

In the Old Testament, the sons
usually received their inheritance while their
fathers were still living. Thus, a father was
able to oversee their stewardship
while they were alive.

---

*House and wealth are an
inheritance from fathers.*

Proverbs 19:14

Overflowing Supply

A Christian is in financial bondage
if there is no financial commitment to God's
work. This principle is basic to Christian
financial management.

---

*Honor the Lord from your wealth, and from
the first of all your produce; so your barns will
be filled with plenty, and your vats will
overflow with new wine.*

Proverbs 3:9,10

Quick Depression

If you have a lot of
debt and a get-rich-quick mentality,
you will bring depression into your family.

---

*It is the blessing of the Lord that makes
rich, and He adds no sorrow to it.*

Proverbs 10:22

Only The Essentials

A Christian in debt must
stop any expenditure that is not
absolutely essential.

---

*He who loves pleasure will
become poor; whoever loves
wine and oil will never be rich.*

Proverbs 21:17 NIV

Thou Shalt Not Covet

Covetousness should not
characterize the Christian. Set your
goals and standards based on God's
conviction—not on what others possess.

---

*You shall not covet your
neighbor's wife, and you shall not desire your
neighbor's house...or anything that
belongs to your neighbor.*

Deuteronomy 5:21

Treasured Blessings

The Scriptures give evidence
that prosperity is one of God's
blessings to those who love
and obey Him.

---

*To endow those who love me with
wealth, that I may fill their treasuries.*

Proverbs 8:21

Seek Financial Freedom

Financial bondage can exist not only
from a lack of money or by overspending, but
also from an abundance of money or
misunderstanding why God gave it to us.

Instruct those who are rich in this present world
not to be conceited or to fix their hope
on the uncertainty of riches, but
on God, who richly supplies
us with all things to enjoy.
1 Timothy 6:17

Peace Over Success

God never provides success
at the expense of our peace.

---

*Peace I leave with you; My peace I
give to you; not as the world gives,
do I give to you. Let not your heart
be troubled, nor let it be fearful.*

John 14:27

His—Her—Our Money

Regardless of who makes
the most money, it is essential that you
operate in the "our money" frame of mind—not
"my money" or "her money"
or "his money."

---

*For this cause a man shall leave
his father and his mother, and shall cleave to
his wife; and they shall become one flesh.*

Genesis 2:24

Risking Others' Money

It's one thing to speculate with money you can
afford to lose and quite another to lose money
that literally belongs to another.

---

*A prudent man sees evil and hides himself, the
naive proceed and pay the penalty.*

Proverbs 27:12

Important Fact

At the rate personal bankruptcies grew during the last decade, it is estimated that they will reach four million by the year 2000—and that's with no major economic crisis.

Controlling Conditions

If we make a total transfer
of everything to God, He will
demonstrate His ability. God will
keep His promise to provide every need
we have through physical, material,
and spiritual means, according
to His perfect plan.

You shall walk in all the way which the Lord
your God has commanded you, that you may live,
and that it may be well with you.

Deuteronomy 5:33

A Helpmate's Advice

In God's Word the husband is
warned to treat his wife with grace and honor,
so his "prayers may not be hindered." When a
husband avoids or ignores his wife's counsel on
any matter, including finances, he should
expect his prayers to be hindered.

---

*You husbands likewise, live with your wives
in an understanding way...and grant her honor
as a fellow heir of the grace of life, so that your
prayers may not be hindered.*

1 Peter 3:7

Money-In, Money-Out

Beware of the more-money-in,
more-money-out syndrome. This means you
spend more simply because you have more.

---

*If riches increase, do not set
your heart upon them.*

Psalm 62:10

Fast Cycles

Much debt exists because it
seems faster and simpler to borrow
than to save. Most of our economic cycles
can be traced directly to the availability,
or the lack of availability, of credit.

---

*The plans of the diligent lead surely
to advantage, but everyone who is
hasty comes surely to poverty.*

Proverbs 21:5

Monthly Monitoring

After you have determined
what you should be spending on
each category every month, the next step is
to monitor your monthly spending.

---

*Know well the condition of your flocks,
and pay attention to your herds.*

Proverbs 27:23

Test The Counsel

Select good investment
counselors based on the following criteria.
Test their counsel, compare it to God's Word,
test their value systems, look at their track
records, and ask for references.

---

*Plans fail for lack of counsel,
but with many advisers they succeed.*

Proverbs 15:22 NIV

Valuable Counselors

Select your counselors on the
basis of a common value system. For the
Christian, that means to choose those
who acknowledge Jesus Christ as
their Savior and Lord.

---

*How blessed is the man who does not
walk in the counsel of the wicked,
nor stand in the path of sinners,
nor sit in the seat of scoffers!*

Psalm 1:1

Don't Be Naive

The purpose of counsel is to offer suggestions,
alternatives, and options—
not to make your decisions.

The naive believes everything,
but the prudent man considers his steps.

Proverbs 14:15

Dangerous Egos

Many Christians have had their egos
shattered by financial setbacks. Some respond
by panicking, to the point that they abandon
their Christian principles and cheat and lie to
protect their security. Others accept God's
authority over their lives and use this as an
opportunity to trust God more fully and
to demonstrate to others that they serve God.

---

*Through all this Job did not sin nor
did he blame God.*

Job 1:22

Necessities and Whims

If you believe a purchase is
within God's will, you will have peace.
But if you assess that the purchase is a desire
or whim, stop to check God's principles.

A tranquil heart is life to the body,
but passion is rottenness to the bones.

Proverbs 14:30

Avoid Competition

Because we are in a competitive society
we often determine people's worth by
their ability to buy things.

---

*For what will a man be profited, if he gains the
whole world, and forfeits his soul?*

Matthew 16:26

A Critical Spirit

When a believer is living a lifestyle
that is contrary to God's way, the step from
hypocrisy to a critical spirit is a short one.

Put away from you a deceitful mouth,
and put devious lips far from you.

Proverbs 4:24

Kingdom Efforts

Service to Jesus Christ is demanding.
It may actually mean that we have to
work as hard for God's kingdom
as we do for earthly riches.

He who loves his life loses it; and he
who hates his life in this world shall
keep it to life eternal.

John 12:25

Business Foundations

One long-range goal of every
Christian businessperson should be to become
debt-free. God never promises quick growth;
He promises a solid foundation.

---

*He is like a man building a house, who dug
deep and laid a foundation upon the rock; and
when a flood rose, the torrent burst against that
house and could not shake
it, because it had been well built.*

Luke 6:48

Humble Callings

Quite often, putting God first in the
area of vocation will necessitate choosing a
vocation that has little or no retirement
security or ego-building status.

---

*And the one on whom seed was
sown among the thorns, this is the man who
hears the word, and the worry of the world,
and the deceitfulness of riches choke the
word, and it becomes unfruitful.*

Matthew 13:22

Inviting Traps

Never allow yourself to be trapped
into anything that is unethical, immoral,
or dishonest, no matter how inviting it seems.

---

*Better is a little with the fear of the Lord,
than great treasure and turmoil with it.*

Proverbs 15:16

Budgeting The Card

A working budget must be a prerequisite
to the use of credit cards. Without a budget,
there is no meaningful context to determine if a
particular purchase can be afforded.

---

*Therefore be careful how you walk,
not as unwise men, but as wise.*

Ephesians 5:15

Slipping Away

Becoming content without God in our
abundance is a much more subtle sin than
stealing. We just slip outside of God's will and
never realize it until calamity hits.

---

*Feed me with the food that is my
portion, lest I be full and deny Thee
and say, "Who is the Lord?"*

Proverbs 30:8,9

Saving Wives

A spender is balanced by a saver.
A sensitive, discerning wife is a great
asset to any husband, providing that
he's willing to listen to her.

A prudent wife is from the Lord.

Proverbs 19:14

The Pressure To Consume

To stand against the pressure to
buy and consume in our culture is as
hard as trying to stand still in an ocean with
hurricane tides. For one individual or couple
to do it alone is nearly impossible.
We need each other.

---

*Two are better than one because they have
a good return for their labor. For if
either of them falls, the one will
lift up his companion.*

Ecclesiastes 4:9,10

Tithes That Prosper

God's Word describes the tithe as a testimony
to God's ownership. It was through the tithe
that Abraham acknowledged God's ownership.
Thus, God was able to direct and prosper him.

---

*And blessed be God Most High, who has
delivered your enemies into your hand.
And he gave him a tenth of all.*

Genesis 14:20

Poverty No Virtue

Some people think that "poverty
is next to spirituality." Wrong!
There is no inherent virtue in
poverty. There are dishonest
poor just as there are dishonest rich.

---

*The rich and the poor have a common
bond, the Lord is the maker of them all.*

Proverbs 22:2

The Material World

Christ warned us a great
deal more about materialism
than He did about any other sin.

---

*Beware, and be on your guard
against every form of greed; for not
even when one has an abundance does
his life consist of his possessions.*

Luke 12:15

Liars And Thieves

The liars and the thieves will
cheat those who obey godly principles,
and it is quite possible that the ways of
the wicked will cause them to prosper.
A Christian must remember that all
that is seen is not all that there is.

---

*The wicked earns deceptive wages, but he who
sows righteousness gets a true reward.*

Proverbs 11:18

Balanced Families

Each Christian family must
decide on the level God has planned
for them and stick to it in spite of available
surpluses. Remember that balance is essential.
Too much spending breeds indulgence; too
little is self-punishment.

---

*And whatever we ask we receive from Him,
because we keep His commandments and do
the things that are pleasing in His sight.*

1 John 3:22

No Budget, No Buy

Curb your impulse to buy. If you
haven't budgeted for it, don't buy it.

---

*Like a city that is broken into and
without walls is a man who has no
control over his spirit.*

Proverbs 25:28

A Little At A Time

You should practice saving money on
a regular basis—even if you are in debt. If
you can save no more than $5 a month,
develop a discipline of saving.

---

*A sluggard does not plow in season; so at
harvest time he looks but finds nothing.*

Proverbs 20:4 NIV

Shrewd Dealings

The way someone deals with
creditors says a lot about his or her
character and about their Christian witness.

---

*Make friends quickly with your opponent at
law while you are with him on the way, in
order that your opponent may not
deliver you to the judge...and
you be thrown into prison.*

Matthew 5:25

Resentful Sharing?

Attitudes play an important part in sharing
with others. Have you ever given to someone
resentfully? I have, and almost immediately
realized I had given up more than money.

---

*Let each one do just as he has
purposed in his heart; not grudgingly or
under compulsion; for God loves a
cheerful giver.*

2 Corinthians 9:7

Important Fact

It would shock Americans to realize that a great deal of the economic information being fed their children in schools is blatantly socialistic.

Planning Ahead

Any financial plan for
Christians should be in harmony
with prayer-guided, long-range goals.

---

*For which one of you, when he wants to
build a tower, does not first sit down
and calculate the cost, to see if he has
enough to complete it?*

Luke 14:28

Plan Ahead

Many Christians will suffer
needlessly because of their own foolish
decisions and failure to plan properly,
based on God's Word.

---

*Thy word is a lamp to my feet,
and a light to my path.*

Psalm 119:105

Unimpressive Giving

Giving to impress others does not impress God.
People who have a problem with
pride need to do their giving
modestly and humbly.

When therefore you give alms, do not sound a
trumpet before you, as the hypocrites do...
that they may be honored by men. Truly I say to
you, they have their reward in full.

Matthew 6:2

Don't Wait To Give

People who have a problem sharing with others
need to give more and wait less.

---

*But whoever has the world's goods,
and beholds his brother in need and
closes his heart against him, how does
the love of God abide in him?*

1 John 3:17

Hand Over The Keys

I've found that a key to my sense of
peace and my ability to make clear and
wise choices is consciously to hand over
ownership of my resources to God.

Let a man regard us in this manner,
as servants of Christ, and steward
of the mysteries of God.

1 Corinthians 4:1

Counsel Of Others

It is a wise person who seeks the counsel of others. To find God's direction, God wants us to be open and listen to people with the same value systems.

Without consultation, plans are frustrated, but with many counselors they succeed.

Proverbs 15:22

Complex Advice

The areas of taxes, securities, stocks, bonds, and real estate are so complex today that only with a variety of good counselors can you really get good advice.

He who walks with wise men will be wise, but the companion of fools will suffer harm.

Proverbs 13:20

Discipline Reduces Greed

I find that once a commitment has
been made to a disciplined lifestyle, regardless
of the available income, the dangers of
greed and self-indulgence are significantly
reduced. The term used throughout
Paul's writings is *contentment*.

---

*But godliness actually is a means of great gain,
when accompanied by contentment.*

1 Timothy 6:6

The Best Standard

To avoid financial traps, you must
establish your standards by God's Word: Seek
God's plan for your life, stick with what you
know, seek good counsel, and wait on
God's peace for acting.

---

*For you have need of endurance, so that when
you have done the will of God, you may
receive what was promised.*

Hebrews 10:36

Long-Term Inheritance

In biblical times, the sons inherited
their father's properties and thus
provided for the rest of their family.

---

*A good man leaves an inheritance to his
children's children, and the wealth of
the sinner is stored up for the righteous.*

Proverbs 13:22

Stay Out Of Court

Christians are clearly admonished in
Paul's letter to the Corinthians never
to take another Christian before the
secular court for any reason. That
would certainly apply to the
collection of debts.

---

*Does any one of you, when he has a
case against his neighbor, dare to
go to law before the unrighteous,
and not before the saints?*

1 Corinthians 6:1

Working Resentment

When a wife is compelled to work by
design or circumstance, resentment
will often develop.

---

*A joyful heart makes a cheerful face, but when
the heart is sad, the spirit is broken.*

Proverbs 15:13

Brotherly Interest?

There is little Scripture dealing with the specifics of lending and charging interest, but what there is would seem to be very clear—don't charge interest to your "brothers."

You shall not charge interest to your countrymen: interest on money, food, or anything that may be loaned at interest.

Deuteronomy 23:19

Hoarding In Vain

A Christian cannot be within
God's will and hoard money.

---

*For he sees that even wise men die; the stupid
and the senseless alike perish,
and leave their wealth to others.*

Psalm 49:10

Serve Or Be Served

The accumulation of money is a major deterrent
to a humble spirit. The tendency is to desire to
be served rather than to serve.

---

*Whoever wishes to become great among you
shall be your servant, and whoever wishes to be
first among you shall be your slave.*

Matthew 20:26,27

Don't Love Money

It's not material things that are
the problem; it is materialism.

---

*For the love of money is a root of all
kinds of evil. Some people, eager for
money, have wandered from the faith
and pierced themselves with many griefs.*

1 Timothy 6:10 NIV

Gone In The End

Solomon found that regardless of his
station in life, man accumulates nothing.
A person's wealth and possessions
amount to nothing upon their death.

---

*Do not lay up for yourselves treasures
upon earth...but lay up for
yourselves treasures in heaven.*

Matthew 6:19,20

The Proper Kind Of Welfare

Too often Christian employers are more
intent on making money than providing
for the welfare of employees.

---

*For the Scripture says, "You shall not muzzle
the ox while he is threshing," and
"The laborer is worthy of his wages."*

1 Timothy 5:18

America's Blessings

What we consider to be a minimum standard of
living is significantly above that experienced in
most other parts of the world. It is not unheard
of for someone living on a small fixed income
to accumulate tens of thousands of dollars
through scrimping and sacrificing.

---

*In all labor there is profit, but
mere talk leads only to poverty.*

Proverbs 14:23

Downshift Comfortably

If you have learned to adjust your standard
of living during your income years, then
retirement will be a comfortable adjustment.

He who loves pleasure will become a poor man;
He who loves wine and oil will not become rich.

Proverbs 21:17

Can You Collect?

It is certain that if Christians are involved
in lending to any extent, especially in business,
they will be tested in the area of collecting.

---

*Then summoning him, his lord said to him,
"You wicked slave, I forgave you all that debt
because you entreated me. Should you not also
have had mercy on your fellow slave, even
as I had mercy on you?"*

Matthew 18:32,33

Pray About It All

God cares about the house you live in, the car
you drive, where you work, whether your wife
should work, your children's college, and even
the food you eat. Have you ever prayed
about those things?

---

*I will cry to God Most High, to God
who accomplishes all things for me.*

Psalm 57:2

An Honorable Price

Should a Christian in business, whether offering
a factory product or a doctor's services, charge
what the market will bear? Wouldn't it be a
testimony to the Lord and His people if
Christians established prices and fees
on the basis of what is fair both
for them and their customers?

---

*Better is a little with righteousness
than great income with injustice.*

Proverbs 16:8

God Leads In Lack

Too often we believe God will direct our lives
only through abundance of money, and we keep
probing to see where He supplies it. However,
through the lack of money, God will steer us
down His path just as quickly.

---

*Give me neither poverty nor riches; feed
me with the food that is my portion, lest I be
full and deny Thee and say, "Who is the
Lord?" Or lest I be in want and steal,
and profane the name of my God.*

Proverbs 30:8,9

Sincere Signs

The tithe was established as a physical, earthly demonstration of man's commitment to God. God understood our greedy, selfish nature and provided an identifiable sign of our sincerity.

But seek first His kingdom and His righteousness; and all these things shall be added to you.

Matthew 6:33

Good Habits

Establish a habit of giving.
Above the tithe God wants Christians
to be involved with the needs of others.

---

*Truly I say to you, to the extent that you did
it to one of these brothers of Mine, even the
least of them, you did it to Me.*

Matthew 25:40

The "You-Owe-Me" Attitude

As a Christian employee, consider whether
your actions are different from the "you-
owe-me" attitude commonly found
in the workplace today.

---

*With good will render service, as
to the Lord, and not to men.*

Ephesians 6:7

The Greatest Threat

It is clear from God's Word that
affluence presents the greatest threat
to our walk with the Lord.

---

*Where your treasure is, there
will your heart be also.*

Matthew 6:21

Control Your Own Spending

Some couples become legalistic and try to control their spending right down to the nickel. Unfortunately, many times it's the husband or the wife trying to control the other's spending.

Love....does not act unbecomingly; it does not seek its own, is not provoked, does not take into account a wrong suffered.

1 Corinthians 13:3,4,5

Family Troubles

In counseling, I find that as many
as 80 percent of Christian families today
either suffer from overspending or have suffered
from it in the past. That is partly because
families have no plan for their finances
and continue to borrow beyond
their ability to repay.

---

*He is on the path of life who heeds
instruction, but he who forsakes
reproof goes astray.*

Proverbs 10:17

Let The Borrower Beware!

If one must borrow outside of God's
people in order to do His work, beware! That
is not according to His plan.

---

*The rich rules over the poor, and the borrower
becomes the lender's slave.*

Proverbs 22:7

Important Fact

The average credit card company in the United States allows an individual to borrow 250 percent more than he or she can conceivably pay.

Suit Yourselves?

I would like to be able to tell you that by giving up the right to sue, God will intervene to recover the material assets lost, but no such promise is made in God's Word. God may choose to do so—but He may also choose not to.

And someone in the crowd said to Him, "Teacher, tell my brother to divide the family inheritance with me." But He said to him, "Man, who appointed Me a judge or arbiter over you?"

Luke 12:13,14

Partial Savings

Simply put, wise people
save a part of their earnings.

---

*There is precious treasure and oil
in the dwelling of the wise, but a
foolish man swallows it up.*

Proverbs 21:20

The Productive Years

Storing some funds during the
most productive years of your life for
the later years is both logical and biblical.

---

*Go to the ant, O sluggard, observe her
ways and be wise, which, having no
chief, officer, or ruler, prepares her
food in the summer, and gathers
her provision in the harvest.*

Proverbs 6:6

Out Of Balance

We seem to be a society of extremes.
We borrow, spend, and work excessively
during our early years—and then
we want to quit altogether.

---

*O naive ones, discern prudence;
and, O fools, discern wisdom.*

Proverbs 8:5

Pledging The Future

Surety means to deposit a pledge in either money, goods, or partial payment for a greater obligation. Surety means taking on an obligation to pay later without a certain way to pay.

A man lacking in sense pledges, and becomes surety in the presence of his neighbor.

Proverbs 17:18

121

The Right Attitude

To avoid financial superiority a Christian must apply the attitude God shows us in His Word.

———————————

Do nothing from selfishness or empty conceit, but with humility of mind let each of you regard one another as more important than himself; do not merely look out for your own personal interests, but also for the interests of others.

Philippians 2:3,4

A Continual Supply

Share with those in need in your time
of plenty, that in your time of need they will
be willing to share from their plenty.

---

*At the present time your plenty will
supply what they need, so that in turn
their plenty will supply what you need.*

2 Corinthians 8:14 NIV

Sharing With Others

It is the responsibility of
Christians to supply the needs of
others who cannot do so for themselves.

---

*If a brother or sister is without clothing
and in need of daily food, and one of you
says to them, "Go in peace, be warmed and be
filled," and yet you do not give them what is
necessary for their body, what use is that?*

James 2:15,16

Start Early

Early goal setting will go a long way
toward eliminating insecurities
and frustrations later in life.

---

*A plan in the heart of a
man is like deep water, but a
man of understanding draws it out.*

Proverbs 20:5

Envious Lifestyles

We are not to envy those who are storing
up riches. Unfortunately, it is easy to fall
into this trap. We begin to envy others and
allow our lifestyles to be dictated
by those around us.

---

*It is better to be of a humble spirit
with the lowly, than to divide the
spoil with the proud.*

Proverbs 16:19

Know Your Risks

Risk is not necessarily bad, as long as you know what the probable risks are and can afford to assume them. The less you know about the investments you make, the harder it is to assess this risk.

A man of understanding delights in wisdom.

Proverbs 10:23 NIV

Material Idolatry

What is an idolater? One who
puts material possessions before God.

---

*No immoral or impure person or covetous man,
who is an idolater, has an inheritance in the
kingdom of Christ and God.*

Ephesians 5:5

Taxes Are For Everyone

Paul was specific in his instructions
concerning the payment of taxes.

---

*Render to all what is due them: tax to whom
tax is due; custom to whom custom; fear to
whom fear; honor to whom honor.*

Romans 13:7

Tough Times

Businesses ride their creditors to the limit,
believing that it is easier to owe someone else
than to cut back during tough times.

---

*Do not withhold good from those
to whom it is due, when it is in
your power to do it.*

Proverbs 3:27

Calming The Creditors

Many people who feel they can't pay a bill will avoid the creditor out of embarrassment. Many times a well worded letter or phone call stating your willingness to work out a reasonable repayment plan will help to restore the relationship.

A gentle answer turns away wrath, but a harsh word stirs up anger.

Proverbs 15:1

Undeserving Love

Material blessings were given because God
loved His people, not because they deserved
them. They were withdrawn from those who
used them foolishly and transferred to
a more faithful steward.

You ask and do not receive,
because you ask with wrong motives,
so that you may spend it on your pleasures.

James 4:3

Don't Cross The Line

Take maximum advantage of every
tax law in existence: charitable giving, tax
sheltering, depreciation, expenses, and any
other step. But be careful not to cross the line
and become involved in tax evasion and theft.

He who profits illicitly
troubles his own house.

Proverbs 15:27

He Wrote The Laws

God wrote the rules of business economics, and,
through the ages, those who followed God's
path have prospered while bringing countless
lost souls into God's eternal family.

---

*For its profit is better than the profit of silver,
and its gain than fine gold. She is more
precious than jewels; and nothing
you desire compares with her.*

Proverbs 3:14,15

Never Too Much

It is better to be wrong and give too much than to ignore God's direction and give too little. The spirit is never dampened by being too sensitive, only by developing callousness.

Therefore openly before the churches show them the proof of your love and of our reason for boasting about you.

2 Corinthians 8:24

Everyone Is Different

God never intended for everyone to give the same amount or in the same way, but each should give bountifully and cheerfully.

He who sows sparingly shall also reap sparingly; and he who sows bountifully shall also reap bountifully. Let each one do just as he has purposed in his heart; not grudgingly or under compulsion; for God loves a cheerful giver.

2 Corinthians 9:6,7

Key Questions

"How will I ever be able to send my child to college?" "What will I be able to do about retirement?" There are no simple answers to these questions except what the Lord said.

Therefore do not be anxious for tomorrow; for tomorrow will care for itself.

Matthew 6:34

Organized To The End

One of the most important things
you can do is to make a list of where your
important papers are and what to do
in the event of your death.

---

*The days of the blameless are known
to the Lord, and their inheritance
will endure forever.*

Psalm 37:18 NIV

When To Retire?

It may be company policy to retire at
sixty-two or sixty-five. But it may also
be that the decision is totally under
your control, and you shouldn't retire.

---

*For by me your days will be multiplied,
and years of life will be added to you.*

Proverbs 9:11

Active In Service

Perhaps the best retirement plan of all
is to learn a service skill that others need.

---

*So in everything, do to others what
you would have them do to you.*

Matthew 7:12 NIV

Over Insured

The desire for protection is displayed through storing large hoards of life insurance, disability insurance, liability insurance, or massive amounts of assets. Understand, none of those are bad in themselves; it is only through misuse that they become corruptive.

Where your treasure is, there will your heart be also.

Matthew 6:21

Stick To The Plan

We must believe that God wants to bless us, and, until God individually convicts someone that His plan is otherwise, we are not to accept failure.

Commit to the Lord whatever you do, and your plans will succeed.

Proverbs 16:3 NIV

Do What You Can

Too often it's a Christian cop-out to declare,
"We're just supposed to trust the Lord."
Certainly we are, but we should also do all we
can to help solve the problems.

---

*"A little sleep, a little slumber, A little folding
of the hands to rest," then your poverty
will come as a robber, and your
want like an armed man.*

Proverbs 24:33,34

Whose Standards?

Are your decisions made by worldly
standards—security, ego, income—or
are they made to please and serve God
and thus serve other people?

---

*He who loves money will not be satisfied with
money, nor he who loves abundance with its
income. This too is vanity.*

Ecclesiastes 5:10

Divide Your Eggs

An old adage says, "Don't put all your
eggs in one basket"; that certainly applies
to your investment strategy.

---

*How blessed is the man who finds wisdom,
and the man who gains understanding.*

Proverbs 3:13

Trinkets Or Great Treasures?

We settle for trinkets now when God really
desires to pour out His blessings upon us.

---

*See if I will not throw open the floodgates of
heaven and pour out so much blessing that you
will not have room enough for it.*

Malachi 3:10 NIV

Uncertainties Of Life

There are no sure things economically,
and God's Word anticipates that.

---

*Know well the condition of your flocks,
and pay attention to your herds; for
riches are not forever, nor does a
crown endure to all generations.*

Proverbs 27:23,24

Important Fact

Nearly 80 percent of divorced couples between the ages of twenty and thirty state that financial problems were the primary cause of their divorce.

God In Your Business

Acknowledge and obey God's eternal
wisdom in operating your business. In other
words, seek God's counsel first.

---

*If the Lord delights in a man's way, he makes
his steps firm; though he stumble,
he will not fall, for the Lord
upholds him with his hand.*

Psalms 37:23,24 NIV

Family Versus Career

God never provides
success at the expense of the family.

---

*It is vain for you to rise up early, to retire late,
to eat the bread of painful labors; for He gives
to His beloved even in his sleep.*

Psalm 127:2

He Meets Our Needs

While God expects us to provide for our families and allows no attitudes of laziness, He also supplies every one of our needs.

And my God shall supply all your needs according to His riches in Christ Jesus.

Philippians 4:19

Three Together

Sometimes it is easier to commit our money than it is to commit our time and talent. I find that a stewardship commitment involves all three.

Be shepherds of God's flock that is under your care...not because you must, but because you are willing...not greedy for money, but eager to serve.

1 Peter 5:2 NIV

It's Paid For!

The one nonvariable is this: What you
own belongs to you and not to a lender.

---

*Owe nothing to anyone except
to love one another.*

Romans 13:8

Secrets of Contentment

Contentment is *not* being satisfied where
you are. It is knowing God's plan for your life,
having the conviction to live it, and believing
that God's peace is greater than the
world's problems.

The righteous will be remembered forever.
He will not fear evil tidings; his heart is
steadfast, trusting in the Lord.

Psalm 112:6,7

Just Passing Through

You actually don't own anything in the
long-term sense; you are just managers.
You know that you can't take anything
with you at death.

---

*For we have brought nothing into the world, so
we cannot take anything out of it either.*

1 Timothy 6:7

Generational Provisions

It becomes obvious that the same promises God
makes about lifetime provisions extend from
generation to generation.

---

*I have been young, and now I am old;
yet I have not seen the righteous forsaken,
or his descendants begging bread.*

Psalm 37:25

Sold Out For God

God's Word promises that He owns everything
and that He delights in helping those who
completely sell out to Him.

---

*For the eyes of the Lord move to
and fro throughout the earth that
He may strongly support those
whose heart is completely His.*

2 Chronicles 16:9

About the Author

Larry Burkett, founder and president of Christian Financial Concepts, is the best-selling author of two novels and fifty-one books on business and personal finance. He also hosts two radio programs, which are broadcast on hundreds of stations worldwide.

Larry holds degrees in marketing and finance, and for several years served as a manager in the space program at Cape Canaveral, Florida. He also has been vice president of an electronics manufacturing firm. Larry's education, business experience, and solid understanding of God's Word enable him to give practical, Bible-based financial counsel to families, churches, and businesses.

In 1976, Larry Burkett founded Christian Financial Concepts as a nonprofit, nondenominational ministry dedicated to helping God's people gain a clear understanding of how to manage their money according to scriptural principles. The purpose of CFC is simply to bring glory to God by freeing His people from financial bondage so they may serve Him to their utmost.

One major avenue of this ministry involves training volunteers in budget and debt counseling, then linking them with financially troubled individuals or families through a nationwide referral network. CFC also provides financial management seminars and workshops for churches and other groups.

For further information, please write to:

Christian Financial Concepts
P.O. Box 2377
Gainesville, GA 30503-2377

Additional copies of this book and
the following other portable book
titles from Honor Books are available
at your local bookstore:

God's Little Instruction Book (series)

Martin Luther's Little Instruction Book

Dwight L. Moody's Little Instruction Book

John Wesley's Little Instruction Book

Tulsa, Oklahoma